THE CROOKED TREE

Kaylee E Burns

The Crooked Tree
Copyright © 2021 by Kaylee E Burns

All rights reserved. No part of this publication may be reproduced, distributed, or transmitted in any form or by any means, including photocopying, recording, or other electronic or mechanical methods, without the prior written permission of the author, except in the case of brief quotations embodied in critical reviews and certain other non-commercial uses permitted by copyright law.

Tellwell Talent
www.tellwell.ca

ISBN
978-0-2288-0485-7 (Paperback)

A long time ago in a forest of trees,
Lived a little green spruce with needles for leaves.
He looked quite lovely, well that's what he thought,
Except that his trunk was tied in a knot.

He couldn't remember what made him that way,
But it couldn't be fixed so that's how he stayed.
All the trees in the forest were straight and tall,
But poor little spruce was crooked and small.

The big trees would tease him, "You're just a joke!"

"You'll never be perfect like the Pines and the Oaks"

"Maybe they're right," he started to think.

"I'm nobody special, just a tree with a kink."

Not so far away, in a clear patch of land.
A man started working on what he had planned.
"I want a house, I'll make it from wood,
And the trees in this forest will work very good."

So day after day he came with his saw,
Looking for trees without any flaws.
Down went the Oaks and down went the Pines.
But only the ones that were straight, tall and fine.

Then one day he finished, the house was all done,
And the short little spruce was the very last one.
"Should I cut it down?" He thought to himself.
"It can't be a table and it can't be a shelf."

"I think I will leave it, I don't need another.
Besides, that big knot would just be a bother."
Now that made the spruce very thankful to be,
Not a table or chair, but a small crooked tree.

Draw your best tree!

Draw your best tree!

www.ingramcontent.com/pod-product-compliance
Lightning Source LLC
LaVergne TN
LVHW071733060526
838200LV00031B/485